I0149628

All Scripture references taken from the KJV of the Holy Bible, unless otherwise indicated.

The Mystery of the Mulberry Tree: Deliverance from the Strongman *by*

Dr. Marlene Miles

Freshwater Press 2024

ISBN: 978-1-963164-24-4

Paperback Version

Table of Contents

The Mystery
of the
Mulberry Tree:
Deliverance from the Strongman

Freshwater

Introduction

This is not a fairy tale, nor is it made up. It is a mystery because no one suspected that a mulberry tree could cause so much damage except for the messy fruit that falls from it, in season.

Trees are meant for our good. The fruit is to feed us, with the wood we can build shelter, and the leaves on the trees not only grant us shade, but they are also for the healing of the nations.

The LORD God planted a garden eastward in Eden, and there He put the man whom He had formed. And out of the ground the LORD God made every tree grow that is pleasant to the sight and good for food. The Tree of Life was also in the midst of the garden, and the Tree of the Knowledge of Good and Evil, (Genesis 2:8-9). The Garden was perfect, until Satan got there and put it all in disarray. Then he perverted the trees and use of the trees.

Who would suspect a tree?

Exactly.

That's how trees sponsor serious issues in the lives of many people--, even generational battles, when manipulated by evil men, or women because no one would suspect a *tree.*

Abram went to a tree called the oak of Moreh in a Canaanite oak grove. It was common for religious cults to use trees, to seek messages from their *gods.*

A tree is chosen because it can live for hundreds of years and while it lives, generational battles unfold in its victims.

The Message

This book began because of a dream. As I woke up, I knew that dream was so much more than just a dream. His name was not Elmo, but in this book that is who he is. I almost never dream of Elmo, but in this dream he was one of the main characters.

It was very early morning--, predawn. I had slept for a few hours and then woke up and resumed work on something that was on my mind, or in my spirit. That was my pattern if I woke up very early, I'd write, work on a book, work on a prayer, read, or pray some more. I had saturated myself and my home in prayers. That morning, I had commanded the morning, and the day since it was already the next day, and no longer night.

Because I had the day off from my regular job, I was afforded the luxury of returning to bed and resuming sleep.

In those days I worked in my profession outside the home, but, at home, I did Holy-Spirit led work that I felt mandated to do because I felt slack and guilty, even disobedient for not doing this type of work for the past many years. I was trying to catch up, do my part to redeem the time and help God restore the years that the locusts, and *casual life* (**sin**) had eaten up.

I was repentant and thankful to be able to do this work, and being as diligent as possible to pray, read the Bible, and write as the Holy Spirit led.

Season of War

One of the reasons I became spiritually diligent was because of the attacks. I was in a season of war—mostly because of my *casual* lifestyle. For that reason, I penned the book, **Seasons of War** to help anyone who might be going through the same, anyone who might read it or need it to prepare just in case a spiritual war broke out in their life. One certainly broke out in mine.

You may be one of those people.

You may be one of those people where it seems in your life you are always in a war, or have always gone through spiritual and/or natural wars. I pray that you're not, because it can be exhausting. It can be exhilarating when you win battles, and with God we will always win, but the battles and wars must be fought, else we suffer, lose out, or fall.

You might be inundated with battles and even wars if you inherited spiritual trouble that your parents and ancestors didn't know how to solve, spiritually. They may or may not have created or helped to create these problems, but definitely they didn't know how to fight, didn't know what spiritual warfare was or how to do it. Else, they would have solved them and not left them to you.

My parents were born and raised Baptist, as were their parents. Up to age 23, I personally had never heard the term spiritual warfare uttered in any Baptist church I had ever attended or been a member of. Baptists, Methodists, and some of those other denominations are so gentle and nice, and kind to one another. And sometimes they are too kind to the devil and to his evil agents.

Non-denominational, Full-Gospel folks, Charismatics, Pentecostals--, call them what you want--, they are warriors, who fight. Well, it was *they* fight until I joined them. Now, *we* fight in the Spirit, and Amen!

Pentecostals believe in all the gifts of the Spirit, and we believe in spiritual warfare. We are the warring branch of saved folks. If others don't join us, then I guess we'll be over here by ourselves doing battle. We are the soldiers in the Army of the Lord.

The Saturation

To saturate my home and atmosphere with prayer, in addition to praying hot, fire, judgmental, violent, and dangerous warfare prayers, I kept multiple prayers playing in my home, even while I slept. I did this because one night I fell asleep playing a certain prayer and I was visited by some *entity* that first asked, then begged me to turn it off. This is the first time I was aware of this type of "visitation," and it was not pleasant; it was for some nefarious reason.

It called *itself* my husband.

I had no husband in the natural at that time.

The prayer that the *thing* begged me to turn off was ***The Crying Blood of Jesus***, https://www.youtube.com/watch?v=PIrsrAcC17o&t=1382s so I made sure to loop it and leave it playing every night for months. Not only that, I played it and other prayers and the Word of God while I was at work, saturating my atmosphere. In addition, I had on ***Warfire, The Blood of Jesus, Pass Over,*** and ***Give Us This Day***. Yes, all of those. Prayers are fighting words!

https://www.youtube.com/watch?v=gL-P-O14oSo&t=4036s
https://www.youtube.com/watch?v=hZ9FOFiDZVU

https://www.youtube.com/watch?v=slw_ouEF4-0&t=4606s

https://www.youtube.com/watch?v=j2HcoJv7GXM&t=24139s

I had all those prayers playing on multiple devices –, not loudly, it doesn't have to be loud to be heard in the spirit.

Didn't God come to Elijah in a still, small voice? If you don't choose what to saturate your environment with, it will be chosen for you.

Okay then, so, I finally went back to sleep.

I cannot say I began to dream; I would rather say, the dream began somewhere in the next four hours that I slept.

Elmo

I had a very long dream of Elmo. In the dream, someone I believe to be his twenty something year old daughter was yelling at him telling him that he is selfish and narcissistic, stubborn, because he is not married.

He was lying down in bed, I was beside him, platonically, although I had dated and was in sin with Elmo for too long, which had been a part of my *casual* lifestyle. His daughter was on the opposite side of him telling him that to not get married is evil. She also told him where she would be that night, sleeping in the *wealthy* section of some place, a club? A gym? The Y? I don't know where. But she was letting him know that the expensive things of this world are what she deserves and will have.

Of note here, Elmo's relationship with his daughter, in the natural is about the worst I've seen between a father and daughter. Further, neither this girl nor her father are spiritual, at all.

The dream continued...

While she was talking, I sat up in the bed--, yeah, also in the bed, and agreed with her saying that the whole purpose of coming to Earth *is* to get married. She agreed with me as I bolstered her argument. Because of their horrible relationship she loved to argue with him.

Then the dream conversation became about some woman Elmo was interested in. Feeling no emotion in the dream, about this, I then said, *"Well, why am I still here? I should have been gone if you are trying to be with her. How will you explain me to her?"*

From there, the scene changed...

The Mulberry Tree

From where I was, I turned my head slightly to the right and saw the huge mulberry tree at Mrs. T's house. It dominated the scene and the dream. It was unbelievable, so I took a picture of it—several pictures, actually. This was a backward dream on many levels. That was a childhood tree and scene. I no longer date Elmo, I no longer would have any conversations with his daughter, and I no longer sin, at least not blatantly obvious sin, and especially not ritual sex. No fornication; no adultery, nope, it ain't happening.

My attention and eyes were captured by the mulberry tree of my youth. It was majestic, but grey--, all bark, and had absolutely no leaves on it. I told them that is a mulberry tree that we used to get mulberries from when we were kids. They didn't care or hear or understand what I was talking about, as they are not saved or spiritual. We also don't share the same culture so they might not know what a mulberry is, and if they do, it is probably called by some other name.

Elmo is the reflection of the *nice* strongman. Elmo has no leaves, no fruit; he is gray now. Elmo is the *nice* strongman. Ladies, there are lots of those. (All the men come in these places, and they are all the same...you don't look in their faces, you don't even ask their name... *Tina Turner*). The men who have no defined spirituality and faith in God who are being used by the devil to interrupt or derail a woman's life are all the same in that the *spirits* in them are basically, all the same.

The NICE strongman is still a strongman, he is a blocker, a *blocker spirit.* You let him into your life because he is nice. He is available in almost every way, but he has no plans to marry you. You don't know that he doesn't want to get married; **he** talks about marriage, **he** brings it up. But then that talk quiets down when he starts to get all the things *from you* that a married man gets, without the marriage.

He's not going to marry you, but he blocks you from meeting, dating, and marrying the person you are supposed to be married to, in the natural. He will suck up years and years of your life, if you let him. When he dies, you may be mentioned in his Obit as a faithful companion, as if you are a dog or other pet. That is, if you get mentioned at all. No one in his family considers you family, even if *your* family accepts him, as the woman's family most often does. The man's family covets him and are hard pressed to let him go forth and live his life with the woman of his own choosing. That is probably because of his earning power.

Spiritually, a tree represents a strongman. Keep that in mind as you continue to read.

A Beautiful Woman

With my eyes still on the mulberry tree, I saw in my peripheral vision a beautiful lady come out of the green cape cod house that was next to where the huge, gray fruit tree loomed. She was dressed nicely, as for church. She was familiar to me, I seemed to know her or at least *of* her. She knew me, or *of* me, and also knew that I was seeing her at that time, so I waved at her.

Now, in this vision or dream, I was what I considered my regular size, but I was very large in size related to her. I was large, like the tree, although the tree was larger. She was small like an ant, as it I was hovering over the entire childhood scene as if watching a moving diorama—except for the oversized tree.

The beautiful woman--, I knew her last name, but since she was an adult and I was a child, back then, I didn't know or had ever called her first name. I may have heard my parents mention it— but I didn't know in the dream and don't know what her Christian name is. I'll call her Mrs. T.

Then another nicely dressed lady and a man came out of the house, both she and man waved to me. The second lady was walking back into the house, and she waved at me again. Were they the same lady, in different outfits? Possibly. But I never saw the first lady go back into the house to then come out of the house with the man. In the natural this woman either lived by herself or lived with a husband, but in the dream, this appeared to be the same woman--, Mrs. T going in and out of the house.

I turned my attention from that house and that tree and back to Elmo. The argument with Elmo continued, he didn't say much; he just laid there. I don't remember his face, but I knew it was him as you know something in a dream. It was indicated in the dream that he was interested in someone else, either seriously or not, but I wasn't *it* for him.

Then I said, *What am I supposed to be a side chick? Like* (yeah, I said, **like**) *if she doesn't want you I'm supposed to jump on it. No!*

Then I said, *Or am I your spirit spouse?* No! **Lord forbid!**

Elmo's daughter kept talking, telling him how wrong he was.

I told him that I should have been gone if he wanted to be with someone else. Then, I started crying loudly.

Saints of God, I don't cry. And, I really don't cry dramatically or loudly, so this was out of character for me. But I have noticed, lately, that the Holy Spirit will move me to emotions and tears. It surprises me every time it happens. But normally I don't cry. In this dream, this crying was devoid of emotion, which is something I also don't do. I don't believe in fake crying.

The daughter used my so-called crying as a weapon to yell at her father some more. Then she got on a phone call. While she was on the phone, I kept trying to get her attention because I had thought of something important and wanted to tell her. I tried waving my hands, I tried a lot of things. I even tried to speak Spanish to get her attention. No one in this dream is Spanish or speaks Spanish. So, why Spanish, I don't know.

Now everyone was up and out of bed, standing in that bedroom to engage in this argument, I suppose.

In the dream, I had remembered that the reason Elmo and I are not together is because his sister is a racist and I desperately wanted to tell his daughter, about her aunt and maybe help her to understand why her father is not married, but I couldn't get her attention.

I suddenly woke up. There's a lot to unpack here. I could tell that this was one of those dreams that plans to stick with you, until you sort it all out.

Big Tree, Strongman

Strongmen are rulers of darkness of this world (Ephesians 6:12). They are over every nation, town, and family. A strongman could be assigned over one or more areas of a person's life--, their marriage, career, business, ministry, usually to destroy or shame the person. The strongman stands guard over whatever was stolen from a person to keep that person from having the very thing that is theirs, the thing or things that God has promised and given, or provided for them. It's like a bad game of keep-away where what is yours, is yours, you just don't have it. If it is up to the strongman, you won't have it.

Saints of God, when God shows you something in a dream it is something that He has delivered you from, or is about to deliver you from. Even though, in the dream there is a potentially emotional argument going on with Elmo and his daughter, know that the mulberry tree is the star of this dream, and we must find out why it is there or what it came to tell us. This strongman has to come down and be fully uprooted.

- Every tree working as an evil altar in my life, DIE, in the Name of Jesus.
- Every tree working as an evil altar in my children's life, or in my marriage, or in my career, DIE, in the Name of Jesus.

The Mulberry Bush

Here we go 'round the mulberry bush
The mulberry bush
The mulberry bush
Here we go 'round the mulberry bush
On a cold and frosty morning

This is the way we wash our face
Wash our face
Wash our face
This is the way we wash our face
On a cold and frosty morning

...

This is the way we brush our teeth
Brush our teeth
...

This is the way we comb our hair
...

This is the way we put on our clothes

Here we go 'round the mulberry bush
The mulberry bush
The mulberry bush
Here we go 'round the mulberry bush
On a cold and frosty morning.

Here We Go 'Round the Mulberry Bush appears to be a nursery rhyme, but is actually about England's West Yorkshire Prison. The song is about the required daily walks around the prison yard for female prisoners. The women (and their children supposedly??) would dance around the mulberry tree in the yard for exercise. Prison was not made for women or children, but when women were sent to prison, back then, their children also went to prison. Crime was generational in a very real sense in West Yorkshire. The mother sins, the child pays right along with the mother.

Is this not Scriptural? Yes, it is in ancestral iniquity and generational curses where, if not repented of and forgiven, the children pay for the sins of their ancestors. Usually it's later, though, but in the Shire children paid for crimes along with their mothers.

A prison governor at HM Prison Wakefield, West Yorkshire, England said that the nursery rhyme was about female Victorian prisoners exercising in the yard. The time period is called the Victorian era because of Queen Victoria who reigned Great Britain and Ireland from 1837 until she died in 1901.

So, sometime during those 63 years, a mulberry tree inhabited this prison yard and women inmates would dance around the tree with their children and sing the song. Most likely it was not planted in 1837—, probably before then as they danced around what was already a tree. Every trip around that mulberry tree, singing, or dancing, no matter what they were chanting--, it was worship. It was attention to the tree, and it was worship to the tree. Yes, trees, and other things want worship.

The tree died in May 2019. If planted in 1800 or so, that tree was more than 200 years old when it died.

The mulberry tree in my dream was gray, had no leaves or fruit. It looked old, but mostly it appeared dead, yet was still standing.

Mulberry Tree or Bush?

In many states it is illegal to plant mulberry trees. I have not seen any ordinances where you have to cut one down on your own property if it is already there, but you cannot plant a new one in some areas. Yes, it's because the ripe fruit is messy from a red mulberry tree, but most dangerously, the fruit is poisonous until it is ripe.

We were kids and we knew nothing of the legality or illegality of a mulberry tree. We only knew that every summer we had fruit of every description and none of it was off limits. We ate peaches--, green or ripe, as we chose, from our own family property. We ate green or ripe plums. A favorite was half-ripe plums or apples; we didn't get in trouble with our parents or uncles who grew them. Of course, we didn't let them see we were eating these green fruits, with salt, but it was a sour blast in our mouths that we thought was great.

We had all kinds of fruit trees on our family's land, but this mulberry tree didn't belong to us, or to anyone in our family. It wasn't on our land, so we didn't have access to it, which is good because none of us knew that a green mulberry was poisonous. So, we only had access to it once per year when we were invited to come and take all the ripe mulberries we wanted. Until that invitation came each year, we were so involved with all the other free fruit at our fingertips that we didn't even remember that it existed.

She was a strikingly beautiful woman, the owner of this mulberry tree but from what we knew she was a solitary woman who lived in a neat little Cape Cod house, which wasn't common in our town; most people had ranchers or two-story colonials. Her light green house sat gently on a gently sloping hill. We were invited to come in summer to gather the very juicy fruit, we only had to knock on her door and let her know we were there. Then we'd run rambunctiously to the fruit-laden tree.

Once the mulberries were gathered, we didn't know anything other than to just eat them fresh, many times while still standing under the bushy green tree, sometimes steeped in fallen mulberries that were so messy, sometimes we'd go there barefoot as not to ruin our shoes, especially white Converse or Keds.

The juice of this berry was profuse and like blood, but a deeper purple hue, once it was on anything, it remained. It stained our hands, and we thought it was hilarious the way our lips looked like we had on makeup and even our tongues turned purple. What a tasty treat and a delight to young, country children who were banned from wearing makeup because of our strict but loving, Baptist parents.

It Stands There

Without warning, decades later I dream of the mulberry tree, possibly because I had begun heavy spiritual warfare about three years ago, and I have not let up. Warfare can take time--, seasons.

It stands majestically in the sun but has no leaves. The bark of it is gray and white like an old lady's head, glistening beautifully like the tapestry of a birch tree or an aspen, in fall, but rough.

Naked.

Not a leaf, not a fruit, not a berry. But unashamed standing there proudly unclothed and barren. Like a great harlot--, as an exhibitionist.

Arms upstretched to Heaven, not so much out, but up, like the appendages of a thick gray cactus. Or like a person who is under arrest and their arms are up to be frisked or searched.

Is this indeed the mulberry tree from all those years ago? My dream says it is. It has situated itself right where the mulberry tree of my childhood lavishly grew and bore much fruit. Now, it has imposed itself into my dream. What has it come to say to me? What has it come to say or report? Or, has it come to complain?

With my phone I take a picture of it, thinking that I must because I have to show this to someone, or people--, in the dream I'm thinking of two of my older sisters, to prove that I saw it. It is massively tall, maybe 80 feet tall so I take another picture of it turning the phone to a different angle to be sure I've captured it all on my device. This is a mystery. Why is the tree so big? Yes, to be noticed and not missed. Why am I having such a dream and in the middle of a bedroom brawl, of sorts? Of all the people who know about this tree, who would even believe this?

As I silently muse within the dream, the tree continues to stand guard in the bright glare of the cool, sunny day.

The following is from Judges 6:

The trees went out to anoint a king over them, and they said to the olive tree, "Reign over us."

But the olive tree said to them, "shall I leave my abundance, by which gods and men are honored, and go hold sway over the trees?"

And the trees said to the fig tree, "Come and reign over us."

But the fig tree said to them, "Shall I leave my sweetness and my good fruit and go hold sway over the trees?"

And the trees said to the vine, "You come and reign over us." But the vine said to them, "Shall I leave my vine that cheers God and men and go hold sway over the trees?"

Then all the trees said to the bramble, "You come and reign over us."

And the bramble said to the trees, "If in good faith you are anointing me king over you, then come and take refuge in my shade, but if not, let fire come out of the bramble and devour the cedars of Lebanon. (Judge 9:8-15)

Trees, even trees bask when they have power over others. Everyone wants to be king, even the bramble; he will only accept to be king if he can be *worshipped*. Any power or sway a tree has over man is more desired than to rule over another tree. Man was made to sit in dominion, but the devil would rather anything--, any element of this Earth should take man's dominion. Ultimately the devil wants it for himself, but if the elements would revolt against the plan of God, then man can be taken down.

When what has been put in place to serve you has been programmed to conquer you, you have a real problem. What you do not conquer will conquer you. What you do not defeat will defeat you. What you do not take dominion over, that you're supposed to have dominion over, will take dominion over you. Man, on Earth is the top of the food chain. Do we not know it.

Somebody, tell the trees.

Before

Before the old Mulberry Tree interjected itself into the dream I was listening to a woman tell whom I believe to be her dad that he was a very selfish man because he should be married. She told him the entire purpose of being on Earth was to be married. He was not listening, possibly feigning sleep. Then I said, *"So if you are going to be with her, then what am I supposed to be to you? A side chick? I am not a side chick."*

In the dream I then said, *"A spirit spouse? Do you think I'm a spirit spouse? I am not!"* Right then is when the tree made its visual announcement in the dream.

The two people that I had been talking to in the dream were suspended while I turned my head and attention toward the hulking tree and took pictures of it, and waved at the people who came from the house.

When I came back to the dream conversation, the young lady was on the phone, and I tried everything to get her attention because I had something to tell her; that her aunt is a racist. It was a revelation in the dream, but it wasn't a revelation because I knew that; I've known it for years. I tried everything to get her attention because I didn't want to forget this, and I wanted her so desperately to know it. I even tried speaking a foreign language to get her attention, but she ignored me, intent on her phone, that had a receiver like a landline with cords. This was a real throwback dream, yeah, as back in the day. And, it was the kind of dream that you should throw back, as in a backward dream.

Pray

Pray against demonic dreams; pray against backward dreams. https://www.youtube.com/watch?v=TK Wa5-cm53Q&t=4974s

Any power attacking the staff of my bread, be destroyed, in the Name of Jesus.

Any power attacking my fruitfulness, be destroyed, in the Name of Jesus.

Any power with deep roots, siphoning my water, power, or interfering with the source of my life, be destroyed, in the Name of Jesus.

Any power invoking me to backwardness, die, in the Name of Jesus.

Amen.

Saints of God, there is more to do. We have to do more than cancel an evil or backward dream, but we must do that. We have to interpret the dream and learn from what it may teach us. What in my childhood wants me back there? The tree? Why?

Usually when something is calling you back, it believes you owe it something. Now, that's a clue, because if an idol thinks you owe it something that means that it has probably been taking from you already, perhaps for years, but somehow it can't get any more, so in a dream it shocks you or flags you down to say, *Hey, remember me?* Or worse, *Remember us?* As if this is a love story.

My God of Mercy, it is not.

Have All You Want

We brought our own containers to the mulberry tree for harvesting the berries. We brought bowls or Tupperware. My mother would not allow us to bring a container that was too big, so as not to appear greedy. However, we knew this was our one chance to gather, since we weren't related to Mrs. T, we didn't impose by going back again. We just went that glorious summer day, once a year, when we were invited.

Once there, we could have all we wanted. I remember Mrs. T having said that to us at least once. I recall the shade of that tree with the messy, purple fruit dripping heavily from its branches.

We couldn't bring any containers that were too new as these berries would stain anything, even plastic, ruthlessly. I'm not really sure why that was an issue; I don't think any Tupperware we owned ever had its correct match, except on the day we got it.

Us gathering around that tree every summer and eating that fruit was worship of its own sort, but we had no idea that's what we were doing. We thought we were passing summer days in the country and going on hiking adventures, enjoying tree-picked fruit.

The ripe, heavy mulberries pulled the branches down to Earth, down to us--, we were kids, we weren't that tall yet. The way the purple leaked from the berries onto the ground that was also covered with mulberries. It would be more than a decade before the song came out, but this may have been the **Purple Rain** that the artist formerly known as Prince would sing about. Just as that song was sad, the results of us having all we wanted from that tree came with a price that we also did not know about.

But from what I've learned now, God can bring us out of the evil covenant and DK Olukoya's **Prayer Rain** has the answer for what ails most men spiritually.

Careful, in the natural when you are invited to have all you want--, sometimes a covenant is being formed.

20 Girls

There were as many as twenty girls, over a span of about 10 years, who as adolescents, ate from that tree every summer, at least once, and most often, only once per year because the time that the fruit was ripe was short. Mulberries fall to the ground, or spoil readily in the summer sun. Birds and other animals and insects competed for the mulberries.

Twenty girls, all of them beautiful, lived within walking distance of this mulberry tree.

The girl who lived next door to that house, in her late teens began to become a source of neighborhood entertainment for local men--, even married men whose clandestine visits somehow did not stay secret, though she lived down a long dirt road.

The men bragged; they must have. This girl may have been slow and never should have been taken advantage of, but she was. Often.

She never married, but was often pregnant and having children who also didn't marry. Her youngest brother was mysteriously killed before he was 20 by unknown men because of his dating preference in a hostile racial climate. Her older brother was as mean as cuss and became somewhat of a zombie, but no one knows why, or where he is these days. There are rumors that he is a drug addict. He's the only one in the family who married, but that didn't last long. Soon, he was divorced. The other two never had a chance to marry.

Closest to this tree, on the other side, were two other girls, also very beautiful, who lived with their parents. The oldest one got away. The youngest one seemed fine, but she died so young, was she even 40? This family had 4 really handsome sons who barely married or stayed married.

A bit further away, there were 7 girls. The first got married and shortly divorced, from her abusive husband.

The second was pregnant out of wedlock, allegedly the father of her child died in a boating accident. She married a different man, but then at a young age became widowed after only two or three years of marriage. The siblings of the second man all died in the ocean at very young ages. That man's mother, in another city entirely, had insurance on all the kids, and collected.

The third of the seven got married and shortly after divorced, also from an abusive husband. She married again some years later, then divorced again.

The fourth got married and was shortly after divorced. She married again, and was again divorced from a tumultuous relationship. He liked to argue and had control issues. She married a third time and then divorced.

The fifth married and stayed married.

The sixth married and was shortly after divorced. She married a second time to a belligerent philanderer and became divorced.

The seventh, the youngest, never married, but had two children by two different men.

Further away from where the tree grew there were three other girls. The oldest didn't marry until in her 50's; she appears to still be married.

The middle sister married at about age 30; her husband got cancer and divorced her just before he died so that *his* mother would be his heir, and not his young, beautiful wife.

The last of those three also married late in life and is still married to a husband who shares her passion for staying drunk, high on drugs, or both.

There was a brother who never married; and became physically disabled early in life.

Furthest away from the mulberry tree was another beautiful--, no gorgeous family of all girls, 5 of them, all of beauty queen status.

The oldest had a baby and left the child with her mother and kept living her large city life.

The next married and stayed married.

The next married, had no children, but died young.

The youngest decided to have a baby, no husband.

You might say foundational issues and you might be right except these people were not all related; while there were some familial relations; there were three different bloodlines represented here.

If territorial powers were working here that could make sense that all those people suffered wedlock, divorce, and childbearing issues.

Was there territorial bloodshed that needed to be paid back? The eldest in one of the families loved to insist that women not have babies; she was a big proponent, unsuccessfully, many times of abortion. Yet, it did not stop her from recommending it. Did she have a bloodshed or sacrifice fetish, or did she hate children? *Was she a witch?*

Or, the tree? Perhaps it was the tree. But in my dream the Lord showed me a tree, dead, but still looming large, not a territorial power, and not definitively a witch. He showed me an 80 ft tree that I was sure not to miss, no matter what else happened in that dream.

The woman who lived in the house and owned the mulberry tree was, from this writer's recollection strikingly beautiful. I do not remember meeting any of her husbands, but it was rumored that she had as many as five different husbands. In the dream, she came out of the house alone. Then she came out of the house in another outfit – another day? With a husband. She waved to me, one of the 20 girls as she stepped to her vehicle with her *next* husband.

Mrs. T had one child, a girl from all of those marriages. I never met her because I believe she was much older than I was. Also, each of her 5 marriages was of a short duration.

Five husbands? I remember my dad talking about it, mocking and laughing, but that wasn't funny; it was serious. Did she have five husbands, like the woman that Jesus met at the well? Or did Mrs. T have more than five? The mulberry tree could attest to that, I'm sure the rings in that tree were record of the rings that the owner would wear, and possibly the rings that the 20 girls and 10 neighborhood boys would not wear, or wear for very long.

Perhaps the mystery of that tree is that the rings in that tree are the rings stolen from those very beautiful neighborhood kids who ate and worshipped, or had their marriages stolen from them by that mulberry tree. Their wedding rings…

The black Elizabeth Taylor, I mean she was gorgeous, kept getting husbands, but the visitors who ate of that tree, did not likewise get or keep spouses.

But we wouldn't know any of that until decades later. All we knew is that we were adolescents, and that mulberries were really delicious.

An Enchanted Tree?

We all had pretty great childhoods, so we thought. But years later, if the tree was battling us, all these girls and some or all of their brothers, *why*?

Trees don't just fight people. The tree has to be enchanted, cursed, dedicated to evil and invoked to some mischief or evil by some evil person. In the Wizard of Oz remember all the trees in the enchanted forest were evil. There are evil forests, we think in other cultures, other lands, but how do we know that we don't have evil forests, or single evil trees in our own country? Such as this strongman Mulberry Tree.

All the parents of the 20 girls and their siblings stayed married to their original spouses. As I said, we ate the fruit usually under the tree so we didn't bring much or any home. It's as though, the adults--, well, at least my parents weren't really interested in the mulberries.

But if there are spiritual battles from this tree that didn't start until we were older and had all moved away from home and from that town, the battles could be those of:

- Unattended Altar. There was a time when the one child of Mrs. T. left home for college and to live in the city. As I recall there was a time where the house was empty after Mrs. T had died.
- Unoffered sacrifice
- Violated Covenant
- Broken Dedication
- Curses
- Gates
- Spirit Spouse

- Deities/gods/idols

It doesn't have to be all of those, it could be any one of them. I prayed and asked the Holy Spirit to teach me and tell me about this tree. He helped me solve the anomaly of the one who married who stayed married.

We all grew up and moved away. The one who remained married, #5, made regular treks to our hometown and visited from house to house–, unbeknownst to us. She would be the type to notice land, landscape, trees, and nostalgic things from childhood days. She would be the type, like a Mr. Rogers to go visit the neighborhood and say hello to all the neighbors. She would be the type to notice and give attention to the mulberry tree. As far as any of us know, by invitation, and with permission, she could have been collecting mulberries, when they were in season, for decades from Mrs. T's tree.

The rest of us most likely would not, and did not. She was perhaps the one out of 20 who offered sacrifice to the tree, although she may not have known that was what she was doing. The sacrifice would be attention, and she would be the type to give it.

As far as the programming in the tree, the rest of us who did not continue to visit the tree once per year violated the covenant.

What covenant?

The one we made unknowingly when we went there stood under that tree, ate the mulberries and blabbered on about how good they were. We were praising the tree, that is we were praising the fruit and giving worship. Had we been really saved and wiser we would have thanked JESUS for the fruit and not just have praises floating out there for the tree and whatever powers or deities associated with that tree could grab.

By His hand, we all are fed. We should give thanks to God for the food we eat,

and not thank the food or the tree that grew it.

Where the rest of us, probably according to the tree, probably broke a covenant that we didn't even know was a covenant, or that any covenant was in place, #5, would be the type to honor it--, also unknowingly.

- Lord, in the Name of Jesus, let the anointing that solicits for curses in my life, dry up, in the Name of Jesus.

*Once you worship idols, false gods, deities or demons – as far as they are concerned, you **marry** them.* You didn't go back to renew the covenant every year like you used to? Then that *idol god* is very angry at you. It only takes missing a visit once.

You need Jesus; that is the only way out of this.

God Delivers

As stated, when God shows you a thing in a dream it is sometimes the thing that He is about to deliver you from. He showed me that mulberry tree. That tree is or represents a strongman.

Every tree that bringeth not good fruit let it be hewn and cast in the fire.
(Matthew 7:19)

Adam and Eve were tempted to eat of the Tree of the Knowledge of Good and Evil. Do not sin with the demons that come with sin also come curses, and *familiar knowledge*

Demons know of good and evil because they <u>are</u> evil. They were with

God, so they also know God. This is how they know both good and evil, and they've chosen evil. Once they inhabit your soul, which is immediately after sin, they begin to impart their nature to you.

Every tree that the Lord did not plant should be uprooted, plucked up, hewn down and cast into the fire. Sooner is better than later because trees have roots. The more time they are left to their own devices the deeper and more involved are those roots. That means when you want that tree gone, it will be harder to dislodge.

The "gifts" (counterfeit promises) that come with *idols* are traps and may be embraced by the human and is a way the demons latch on and stay with the person. *Familiar spirit* – people who just "know" things usually celebrate that. God has the real and superior version of that gift, but if a person doesn't know God, they don't know that. We should be seeking Wisdom through the Holy Spirit, not fa*miliar knowledge* from *familiar spirits* because that is psychic 2nd Heaven knowledge.

The knowledge of good and evil is shown to us in the NT. In the Gadarenes, Legion's demons KNEW Jesus whereas the Disciples walking with Him for years were still dense about His true identity. The woman with the familiar spirit cried out the identity of Paul, and Paul cast that spirit out of her.

We need to make our election sure and only take gifts from God through Jesus Christ. When we take gifts from other than God we are most often initiated into some evil covenant or idol marriage.

Yeah, this extends to mulberries, too. It especially extends to food. Truthfully, none of us, no one in that entire neighborhood or town had any idea. We don't even know if the owner of that tree knew. That tree could have already been there when she bought that house. She may have been as confused as we were when her first husband left her. He didn't die, he left. I don't think any of them died. And she was gorgeous. We also don't know what went on in that house, but the woman always appeared quiet, easy tempered, friendly and well put together.

I don't think she knew about or was complicit with that tree.

Still, it is on us to bless the food we eat, thank God for it because by His hand we are fed and continue to be wise and careful about what TREES we eat from. Even now.

The Women, and Their Children

We learned by way of the nursery rhyme that the children were in the West Yorkshire prison with their mothers. The mother was an inmate, and their children were also captives.

The women were introduced to you in a previous chapter. Now, let's go over those again but this time I'll tell you about their children.

The young woman who was used by the men in the neighborhood had three children; none of them married.

The two girls next door married and had one or two children of their own, but recall the youngest of those children, a female died at a young age.

The family of seven girls all had very difficult pregnancies.

1. Had two children, both girls. Two husbands, two divorces.
2. Had two children, both girls; one baby daddy; one husband who died very young.
3. Had one child, a girl by two husbands, two divorces. She married one of the neighborhood boys who also lived next door to the Mulberry Tree. In her early teens she was hospitalized with a heart problem and has lived a life of medical problems ever since.
4. Had no children, but multiple husbands, and multiple divorces.
5. Had four children, all boys; one husband, no divorce. Had a mystery medical emergency as a grade-schooler and rushed to the hospital.

6. Had two children, both girls; two husbands, two divorces.
7. Had two children, both girls; two baby daddies, one dead in a drive by, no husband.

Family of three girls, one boy – the male never married. The oldest girl married in her 50's for the only time, she is still married. The next oldest divorced and widowed at a young age, the third married to a party man, has one child, a girl.

The furthermost neighborhood family, 5 girls, no boys of those parents. Marriages and divorces. One had two girls, who never married or had children. The eldest had two children, both girls. The next died young after suffering some dread disease. The middle girl, gorgeous-- got married and had children. The youngest never got married but had a son out of wedlock (by choice).

Out of all 20 girls I counted 18 marriages, some had multiples, some had none. Of all who had children-- I count about 40+ girls and only 4 boys from the entire group that ate from that mulberry tree.

The average length of a Mulberry Tree Marriage that did not last, was approximately 5 years or less. There were many who never married at all.

I must add one more family who spent summers in that hamlet. They had a girl and two boys. The girl never married and had 5 children by 4 or 5 different men—all girls. Then the 5 girls never married, but they all had multiple children, all girls, except one boy, none of them ever married.

The Fruit

No, I'm not blaming a tree for anything. But those who ate of the fruit of that tree had particularly negative outcomes in relationships, marriage and children, in my opinion. I can't blame the tree; I can only blame the witch or witches who dedicated or charmed the tree. The tree did not and could not do this on its own.

All those bad marriages is noteworthy because they were all the children of **married** parents who were saved, went to church on Sundays, and stayed married to their original spouse of their youth.

What are the patterns of your childhood adventures? What became of your neighbors and neighborhood? Was there a common thing you all did? A common place you all went? A common thing you all ate or drank?

This speaks of collective captivity.

The fruit may be sweet going down but when it gets to the belly is it not bitter? Youthful summers should be well spent, but look at the patterns later in life to see what choices could have been better made. With Jesus Christ as your Lord and Savior, you can pray diligently and be delivered from anything that may have beset you in childhood but has waited until you are a young adult, or an adult to afflict you.

Even a tree.

Not Child's Play

The witches, the evil forest, even all of the Wizard of Oz is about witchcraft – after all a wizard is the title character. We watch it like it's a children's story, but it's all about witchcraft, how is that child's play?

Childhood witchcraft, inadvertent, blind witchcraft--, no matter what kind or how it came about, we can be delivered. When the strongman is found out, he must return all that he has stolen from you. The Holy Spirit, through that Elmo dream has shown me the strongman, that huge mulberry tree.

And it shall be, when you hear the sound of marching in the tops of the mulberry trees, then you shall advance quickly. For then the LORD will go out before you to strike the camp of the Philistines. (2 Samuel 5:24 NKJV)

Abraham planted a tamarisk tree, it was an altar and a tree lives how long? We've learned hundreds of years. An altar lasts how long? As long as it is being serviced, that is as long as offerings, worship are going to that altar it will work.

Witches create effigies or things that represent their victims to manipulate a person, that person's blessings, or that person's life.

- Lord, when a tree is my effigy or when my life is tied to a tree, LORD separate that from me, in the Name of Jesus.

There was only one tree that was cursed in the Bible because it had no figs, no fruit.

- When the strongman is found out he can be spoiled. The Lord has shown me this strongman. We will have to spoil him, in the Name of Jesus.

That tree delayed so many marriages, that took so many marriages, that destroyed so many marriages. Yet the person living there who owned the property had 5 marriages. Was it by her own hand or was it the curse on that land, on that property, that tree?

The Lord said, "If you have faith as a mustard seed, you can say to this mulberry tree, 'Be pulled up by the roots ad be planted in the sea,' and it would obey you. (Luke 17:6)

Mulberry tree, sycamore tree, fig tree, strongman—any kind of tree can be cast down.

Did Jesus not cast every demon out of Legion, and did they not run into the sea? Yes, by way of the swine, but had the swine not been there we would not have seen the outcome of that mighty deliverance. *Be pulled up by the roots and be planted in the sea* – that is telling us that it will live, but there is yet another realm, another kingdom and it is in the sea. There are more living creatures there than we see or think. Also, we know that *spirits* don't DIE as we command them to, we really mean to die out of our lives, die out of our situations.

Pharaoh's army drowned; they cast *themselves* into the sea. Of course, it didn't look like a sea at the time. But let that be a lesson to the world, you can't get what God's people get; you can't do what God's people can do. So, Pharoah and his army cast themselves into the Red Sea. Now that's a mighty deliverance for the Israelites.

It just takes a little bit of strong faith. A mustard seed is hardy, and it grows very hardy plants.

The Lord sees man as the plantings of the Lord. If we look at this battle, the mustard will fight the sycamore. We eat from a fig tree, a mulberry tree, a mustard plant, but there is no fruit on what we know as a sycamore tree that is edible, but there is a tree called the sycamore fig that does bear edible fig fruit. It is most likely the one from the Bible.

The devil can provide for those who seek him, for a season, or seasons, but at a cost of **all**. Everything you get from the devil costs **everything**, even into your generations. Like the worst credit card bill that can never be paid off because it has 14000% interest, extending up to 14 generations.

Mustard trees (bushes) are annuals; they live for only one year--, that seed has to be replanted every year.

While the average sycamore tree generally has a lifespan of 200-400 years in the wild. However, in cultivation, they can live for much longer, with some known to be over 500 years old.

A white mulberry tree can live up to 100 years. Red mulberry trees typically live for 75 years or less. My point is that if there is a dedicated or evil tree tied to you or your bloodline, it will live many generations and cause battle after battle in your bloodline. If you aren't wise, don't know about it, don't fight it, your family may be stuck in misery and defeat.

A sycamore fig tree can grow up to 55 feet tall and has a 20-foot canopy to shadow people, insects, reptiles, rodents. Okay, so the sycamore fig tree is a member of the Mulberry family. It is native to southern Africa and the Arabian Peninsula. It was cultivated in

Israel and Egypt and coveted for its shade, wood, and fruit.

They are neither native to nor actively cultivated in the U.S.

A mature sycamore fig tree will produce up to a ton of figs, pollinated by a fig wasp and bearing four times per year. They are evergreen and begin bearing fruit at year five or six. This is why when Jesus saw the fig tree with leaves, He thought there should be figs because it bears a lot of fruit, and it bears **four times a year**. Most fruit trees can't do that.

The life span of a fig tree may be 500 to 1,000 years; some have been documented to live longer than that, even for centuries.

Like Jesus, we have authority to curse a tree that is not bearing. Additionally, we have authority to curse a tree that is bearing wrong fruit. God hates evil, He hates witchcraft, and He hates perversion. **The tree that looks like a tree, but is a strongman must die, in the Name of Jesus.**

Pakistan Mulberries

Pakistan mulberry trees are faster to bear, they bear fruit in 2 to 3 years after planting. The tree can live several hundred years and still bear fruit as an older tree. I bring this up because Elmo is Pakistani.

Elmo is by no means an arborist or a horticulturist, but he did have a young tree in his front yard when I first met him that he diligently watered. He watered it every day; I think he over watered it. He told me that he watered it so much because his neighbor's tree of the same variety looked so much better. Well, that's Elmo trying to keep up with the Joneses all the time. But looking back, I see that Elmo prospered a lot in that house, but when he moved everything started to change, even deteriorate. As I look back, I wonder if somehow his prosperity was tied to that tree? If it was, I don't have to guess how--, his sister.

After we split up, I had occasion to visit Elmo's living space once and it was peppered with Chinese tokens of luck and prosperity, although he'd never buy anything made in China. Elmo believed in all kinds of luck and things that I never knew he believed in. Looking back, he probably checked his horoscope every day for all I knew. Most likely these items were recommended and possibly sent to him by his sister, who held a lot of influence over him in a lot of matters, either because he didn't want to think on his own, or his sister's witchcraft had started against him. Or against me. Or both of us.

Collateral damage, collective captivity. Elmo's marriage success and marriages were cursed. By being with, sleeping with or married to Elmo, even in the spirit you become one and what happens to Elmo you share in that. This doesn't even take into account what you bring to the relationship yourself, spiritually speaking. So, when you marry a person who has all kinds of curses on them or bad stuff on them, you share in that with them. Even if you don't marry them, but sleep with them, even once, you share in their spiritual *mess,* and they share in yours. When you sleep with a person, you become **one** with them.

If the one you have chosen is not spiritual and are not even trying to break their own ancestral, familial, generational, or individual curses – whether their fault or not, you inherit their problems. Congratulations, you are now a deliverance worker trying to deliver a person who doesn't even want to be delivered. He may not even believe he needs deliverance or that there is a problem, or a spirit world at all. But you're in the heat of the battle doing all the praying, while he watches football.

Every time you sleep with him or her--, you may not even have to sleep with them, it could all transfer to you by association. Every time--, you renew the covenant--, the soul tie, the curses, the mess. This is one of the reasons why and how pain cliques are formed. People become friends because they have the same types of problems or the same painful history. Have they come together to be delivered from their problems, or only to commiserate? If they just commiserate this makes their individual bondage stronger because now the spirits in each of them enforcing the bondage and the yokes are stronger.

As one can put 1000 angels to flight, and two, 10,000 – evil spirits unite as well—if they can get along, they can strengthen their hold on a person or people.

In my dream, Elmo's daughter took a phone call and got distracted because that is who she is in the natural. Yes, she is young, but she is not spiritual. She thinks she's a Methodist and she thinks that's a step up from being a Catholic. **She can't hear me. SHE CAN'T HEAR ME.** Whatever I have to tell her about God, spiritual matters, curses or strongmen, **SHE CAN'T HEAR ME.** As far as she is concerned our conversation is over; she really just wanted to yell at her father, which is part of the curse that family is under.

As long as she is disrespecting her father, it locks the curse in, and she will not respect any male and her marriage(s) or marital life is in jeopardy. She is 33 right now, a beautiful girl--, no spouse. Elmo is unmarried. Elmo's sons are unmarried – all of marrying age.

Elmo's ex-wife is shacked up with an old fling but not married. All those in the dream might as well still be in bed sleeping; they don't see this, and they wouldn't hear it if someone told them. **They've been bewitched,** and I've already told you by whom.

- Pray to the Lord that you have not been bewitched, but if you have, ask Him to break that power over you, I the Name of Jesus. Lord, wake me up, wake me up, spiritually.

Worse, without being spiritual or knowing the why of a thing, the wrong individual usually gets blamed for this. Witches are usually occultic and love to cast blame, it adds to the confusion. Unless deliverance happens, Elmo will be blamed for being unmarried and selfish and Elmo's children, especially the daughter, will blame him.

Now, it is his fault in a sense – the person who put this curse on Elmo is a person he knows but since he doesn't believe in things that he should know about and believe in, he is the perfect victim. Elmo's parents didn't have this problem, it started with Elmo, long before I knew him because a jealous woman in his life wanted to break up his first marriage and she did.

It's his sister. God showed me. It is his sister.

But why would a demon just jack up one marriage when they can steal multiple? There goes the problem. Elmo's sister has two divorces under her belt and Elmo's niece is of marrying age, promiscuous, but no husband.

Elmo's brother's sons do not have this marriage problem, but Elmo's brother's daughter does, but she loves her witchy aunt, having no clue that she is the culprit who is destroying their family by destroying marriages and their generations with her jealousy and witchcraft, and her racism. **Racism is witchcraft**. The Bible says to have no respect of persons.

Prayer—

I pray for myself, my family and Elmo and his, as well as yours, in the Name of Jesus.

I come against every evil covenant, every curse in place because of an evil covenant.

I pray against whatever is keeping myself, my own family, Elmo, and the women in his family, and my family from marrying, staying married and being happy in marriage to break off of them, in the Name of Jesus.

Lord, if the one who put the curse in place is unrepentant, let every curse return back to them and fall on their head and their head alone, in the Name of Jesus. Return to sender, in Jesus' Name.

- Lord, uproot that evil tree and burn its roots to hell in the Name of Jesus.

Show Me My Enemies

If you ask the Lord to show you your enemies, He will. That is, if you are mature enough to know who they are and not dive into the flesh and go off on them.

Soul prosperity is a huge part of spiritual warfare because if you don't know your enemy, you can't see your enemy, if you can't see your enemy how will you fight. The Holy spirit reveals things to you as you are praying, but if you can't handle it, you either won't be told what's happening on the battlefront, or you won't be able to accept the truth and that will delay deliverance and prolong the battle or battles. You need some spiritual maturity about yourself to enter into spiritual warfare. You need the Word in you. The Word will bring prosperity to your soul and to your life.

To appoint unto them that mourn in Zion, to give unto them beauty for ashes, the oil of joy for mourning, the garment of praise for the spirit of heaviness; that they might be called trees of righteousness, the planting of the LORD, that he might be glorified (Isaiah 61:3).

Fire of God

I send the Fire of God to every evil tree that has my name, image, likeness, virtue… to consume every satanic offering that is representing my **life at that altar.**

Any tree growing against my prosperity, catch Fire, in the Name of Jesus.

My peace in marriage that is hidden in any tree, jump out and find me, in the Name of Jesus.

Every tree altar in my family that has the secret of my suffering… Lord, search the land of the living and the dead and find any of my glory from any evil tree and bring it back to me, in the Name of Jesus.

Every tree growing contrary to my marriage that has ever been used to afflict me or affect my life since I was born, let that tree fall, in the Name of Jesus.

Prayer Battle

For the mulberry, the evil tree is exposed. It is cursed. It has no leaves. It is naked. It is ashamed. It is dead and now I will fell it. I will uproot it and cast it into the Fire, and it shall be no more.

The roots of any evil tree shutting down my life, jump out of my life, and catch Fire, in the Name of Jesus.

Satanic trees in the garden of my destiny catch Fire, in Jesus' Name.

The axe is laid unto the root of the trees, therefore every tree which bringeth not forth good fruit is hewn down and cast into the fire, (Mathew 3:10).

You, oh God minister destruction to the ministry of destruction in my family, in the Name of Jesus.

I receive strength and power to be a warrior, and not to be weary, in the Name of Jesus.

I consume the shrine of the strong man in my family with the Fire of God, in the Name of Jesus.

Let stones of Fire pursue and dominate all the strongmen in my life, in the Name of Jesus.

I smash the head of the strong man on the wall of Fire, in the Name of Jesus.

Let hell open its mouth without measure, and swallow all who wish to drain my peace, in the Name of Jesus.

No regrouping, no reinforcement against me by the strongmen in my family, in the Name of Jesus.

Let the Angel of God roll stones of Fire to bowl over every strongman up against me, in the Name of Jesus.

I cause open disgrace to the strongmen in my family. Lord, make an open show of it, in the Name of Jesus.

Let all the enemies of my soul start their days with confusion and end that day in destruction, in the Name of Jesus.

Lord, heal any hormonal imbalance— heal my endocrine system, in the Name of Jesus.

Oh Lord, release my mind from any jealousy, lust and evil intentions, in the Name of Jesus.

Oh Lord, heal me wherever I need to be healed, in the Name of Jesus.

I stand against all confusion forces within me, in the Name of Jesus.

Oh, Lord replace in me whatever needs to be replaced, in Jesus' Name.

Oh Lord, order my inner life. So that I can hear You. Let me see what You see in me.

Lord, transform me in whatever way I need to be transformed.

Lord, let Your healing power be firmly rooted within me, in the Name of Jesus.

Strongman from both sides of my family, destroy yourselves and each other, now, in the Name of Jesus.

I fire back all satanic arrows of discouragement at the edge of breakthrough, in the Name of Jesus.

I fire back all Satanic arrows of spiritual and physical sicknesses, in the Name of Jesus.

I fire back all satanic arrows of weakness in prayer and Bible reading, in the Name of Jesus.

I fire back all satanic arrows of business failure, in the Name of Jesus.

I fire back all evil arrows from the household enemy, in the Name of Jesus.

The strongman from my father's side, my mother's side, began to destroy yourselves, in the Name of Jesus.

I refuse to wear the garment of sorrow, in the Name of Jesus.

All stubborn pursuers in my life, I command you to die, in the Name of Jesus.

All satanic arrows presently in my life, lose your power, in the Name of Jesus.

Let every organized evil arrow against my life be paralyzed, in the Name of Jesus.

I fire back all evil arrows from fake and unfriendly friends, in the Name of Jesus.

Power of God, bring to life all my good benefits that satanic arrows have paralyzed, in the Name of Jesus.

Let the wisdom of all evil counsels in my life be rendered to nothing, in the Name of Jesus.

Oh Lord, cause an explosion of Your power against my enemies, in the Name of Jesus.

Let my life be protected by a hedge of Fire, a wall of fire, a mountain of fire, and let me be soaked and covered with the Blood of Jesus.

Thank You, Lord, that the gate of hell shall not prevail against my life, in the Name of Jesus.

Lord, smite all evil tongues rising up against me, and break the jaw of the evil powers, in the Name of Jesus.

Let every handwriting, contrary to my peace, receive total disgrace, in the Name of Jesus.

Let every decision taken against me by the wicked, be rendered null and void, in the Name of Jesus.

I fire back every demonic arrow targeted at me and my family, in the Name of Jesus.

I break every spiritual mirror and monitoring device used against me, in the Name of Jesus.

I bind and render to nothing all the strongmen that are currently troubling my life. Warrior Angels of God, take them away from my gates, doors, and breakthroughs, in the Name of Jesus.

I disgrace all satanic agents, all water spirits, all satanic prophets, all occultic consultants, the original possessors of my family, all drinkers of blood, eaters of flesh, and the *spirit of sexual perversion*, demonic food sellers selling polluted foods and the bread of sorrow, in the Name of Jesus.

Thank You, Lord.

Let every *power* of every oppressor backfire against them, in the Name of Jesus.

Let my affairs become too hot for the enemy to handle, in Jesus' Name.

I seal every one of my pockets, my basket and my store that has a hole in it, in the Name of Jesus.

I retrieve my blessings from the camp of evil confiscators, in the Name of Jesus.

Let Your power, Your glory and Kingdom come upon my life, in the Name of Jesus.

I vomit every satanic poison in the Name of Jesus.

Let all drinkers of blood and eaters of flesh begin to eat their own flesh and drink their own blood, and DIE, in Jesus' Name.

Let my promotion manifest powerfully, in the Name of Jesus.

I reject temporary freedom in every area of my life, in Jesus' Name.

I reject partial freedom, in every area of my life; Lord, deliver me fully, in Jesus' Name.

Let the joy of the enemy upon my life be turned to sorrow, in the Name of Jesus.

I claim total victory and freedom in all areas of my life, in the Name of Jesus.

Let all bitter water flow out of my life, in the Name of Jesus.

I withdraw all the bullets and ammunition of the enemy; Lord, make him weaponless, in the Name of Jesus.

I bind and paralyze the *spirit of death* and hell over my life, in Jesus' Name.

My name, become Thunder, Fire and Lightning in the ears of those hat call me for evil purposes, in the Name of Jesus.

I decree that there shall be no reinforcement, no regrouping of any strongmen against me, in Jesus' Name.

Unseat the Strongman

The father has given the son authority to execute judgment. If you have become a son of God, stand in your authority and do spiritual warfare for your sake, as well as that of your family and your generations and bloodline.

I order confusion and the scattering of tongues among all the wicked emanating against my peace, in the Name of Jesus.

I bind and render powerless all the strongmen currently troubling me, in the Name of Jesus.

Let the strongman pursuing me drink his own blood and eat his own flesh, and die, in the Name of Jesus.

I render null and void every ritual incantation, spell and curse issued against me by any strongman, in the Name of Jesus.

I disband any wicked meeting held in the spiritual realm against me, in the Name of Jesus.

My life, receive Fire, become Fire (X3), in the Name of Jesus.

Let my office, car and home and everything under my stewardship be too hot for any strongman to handle, in the Name of Jesus.

Lord, waste and cut down every tree of non-achievement in our lives, in the Name of Jesus.

Every failure and poverty mentality has to go, in the Name of Jesus.

Let every tree planted by fear my life dry up from the roots, in the Name of Jesus.

Evil rivers, trees, forest, evil companions, evil pursuers, visions of dead relatives, snakes, *spirit spouse,* DIE, in the Name of Jesus.

Any conscious or unconscious relationship with any spirit spouse, spirit, husband, spirit, wife, die, in the Name of Jesus.

Any idol that thinks I have married it, fall down and die. And that includes any evil tree. Mulberry Tree and the strongman it represents, fall down and die, be uprooted and combust into eternal flames, in the Name of Jesus.

Lord, let every tree not planted by God be rooted out. I uproot and destroy all evil spiritual spouses, in the Name of Jesus.

Lord, let my hand become a sword of Fire to cut down demonic trees in the Name of Jesus.

Every ancestral dedication of children in my family lineage to *idols*, sacred waters, and/or evil trees is broken off my life, in the Name of Jesus.

I will not suffer for the sins of my forefathers; Lord, forgive all iniquity by the Blood of Jesus.

Let every tree of sorrow be uprooted in my life in Jesus' Name.

The problems in my life, dry up to the roots, in Jesus' Name.

Let the Blood of Jesus dry up every evil tree used against me, in the Name of Jesus.

Any evil tree hiding my breakthrough be cursed to the root and then uprooted and cast into the Fire, in the Name of Jesus.

Let all the dead branches in the tree of my life be cut off and be replaced, in the Name of Jesus.

Let any power storing my blessings in any tree, release them, release them, release them, NOW, in the Name of Jesus.

Any tree of profitless hard work, be uprooted, in Jesus' Name.

Trees of evil in my life receive the axe and Fire of God and be uprooted, in the Name of Jesus.

Every stubborn problem tree be uprooted by Fire now, in the Name of Jesus.

Prayer Rain

This is what you are to do to them:
Break down their altars, smash their
sacred stones, cut down their Asherah
poles and burn their idols in the fire.
(NIV)

Every tree in my place of birth harboring
human blood or requiring worship, I
break every evil dedication and
covenant, and command you to catch
Fire, Now and burn to ashes, in the
Name of Jesus.

Every tree of frustration and limitation
in my life, catch Fire in Jesus' Name.

Any power calling my name to any evil
tree catch Fire together with the tree in
the Name of Jesus.

Any sacrifice offered to any tree against me, let the sacrifice backfire and let the tree be struck with the Lightning of God and crash to the Earth, dead, in the Name of Jesus.

Any power nailing my name to any evil tree catch Fire together with the tree, in the Name of Jesus.

Every coven in any tree troubling my destiny, let your *troublings* backfire on your own heads, to utter desolation, in the Name of Jesus.

Any power hanging my blessings on a forest tree, release it and expire, in the Name of Jesus.

Every tree draining my life catch Fire, in the Name of Jesus.

Secret tree serving as a stronghold for my enemies, catch Fire, in Jesus' Name.

Powers that tied my life to a demonic tree leave my life alone, and die, in the Name of Jesus.

Covenant trees of darkness in my destiny, catch Fire, in the Name of Jesus.

Strange pot in a strange tree fighting me, catch Fire, in the Name of Jesus.

Any bitter tree in my life wither by Fire, in the Name of Jesus.

Tree of darkness holding ancestral records against me, catch Fire and every record be completely destroyed by the flames, in the Name of Jesus.

Any power feeding evil trees against me, I place a death notice upon you, in the Name of Jesus: Cease & Desist.

Every ancient tree receiving sacrifices because of me, Sword of God, cut it down, in Jesus' Name.

My virtues, kept in any tree of darkness, come out and locate me now, in the Name of Jesus.

Every tree standing against me on my success journey, Sword of Fire cut it down, in the Name of Jesus.

Strange trees hosting the meetings of wicked elders against me, receive the severe Sword of the Lord, in the Name of Jesus.

I curse that tree of darkness working against my family, my bloodline, my neighborhood, in the Nane of Jesus.

I curse every tree of wickedness in my family, in the Name of Jesus.

As Jesus cursed the fig tree, that tree of the Mulberry family, I curse that Mulberry tree, I curse that tree, I curse that tree, in the Name of Jesus.

Every evil tree assigned against me, I curse it, in the Name of Jesus, Amen.

There is no more enchantment against me, in the Name of Jesus.

Shield of Faith, quench the fire on every fiery dart of the enemy, in Jesus' Name.

Every plant that the Lord did not plant will be uprooted in the Name of Jesus.

I send the Rough Wind of the Lord to uproot any and every evil tree working against me, in the Name of Jesus.

Lord, raise your Rough Wind against every evil altar, working against me, my life, my destiny, my health, and finances, in the Name of Jesus.

Any tree working as an altar in my life, catch Fire, burn to ashes, in Jesus' Name.

The virtues for healing, marriage, destiny helper stolen or stored in any evil tree, release them now, in the Name of Jesus, and then DIE!

Tree of debt growing against my destiny, catch Fire, in the Name of Jesus.

Any evil tree planted in the Garden of my life that wants to kill my destiny, bulldozers from Heaven, uproot and burn it with Fire, in the Name of Jesus.

Spirit of divorce, burn off of my life, in the Name of Jesus.

Witchcraft powers sponsoring divorce, DIE, in the Name of Jesus

I seal these declarations across every dimension, realm, era, age and timeline, past, present, and future, to infinity, in the Mighty Name of Jesus Christ.

Any retaliation because of these prayers, backfire against the enemy 7 times, in the Name of Jesus. **AMEN.**

Thank You, Lord.

I HAVE BOTH GLORIFIED IT AND WILL GLORIFY IT AGAIN...

Instead of the thorn shall come up the fir tree, and instead of the brier shall come up the myrtle tree: and it shall be to the LORD for a name, for an everlasting sign *that* shall not be cut off. Isaiah 55:13

The enemies you see today shall be no more, says the Lord thy God.

Dear Reader

Thank you for acquiring and reading this book. I pray that it has enlightened and strengthened you.

May the Lord break you out of every evil covenant and spiritual marriage. May He *loose* you and your destiny from every evil tree. And, may He restore you to at least sevenfold, all that you have lost and all that has been taken from you.

Dr. Marlene Miles

Other books by this author

AK: The Adventures of the Agape Kid

AMONG SOME THIEVES

Ancestral Powers

Blindsided: *Has the Old Man Bewitched You?*

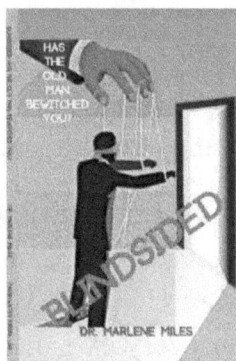

https://a.co/d/5O2fLLR

Churchzilla, The Wanna-Be, Supposed-to-be Bride of Christ

Demons Hate Questions

Devil Weapons: Unforgiveness, Bitterness,…

Dream Defilement

Don't Refuse Me, Lord (4 book series)

Every Evil Bird

Evil Touch

Fantasy Spirit Spouse

FAT Demons (The): *Breaking Demonic Curses*

The Fold (4 book series)

The Fold (Book 1)

 Name Your Seed (Book 2)

The Poor Attitudes of Money (3)

Do Not Orphan Your Seed got HEALING?
Verses for Life got LOVE? Verses for Life got
HOPE? Verses for Life got money?

How to Dental Assist

Let Me Have A Dollar's Worth

Living for the NOW of God

Lose My Location https://a.co/d/crD6mV9

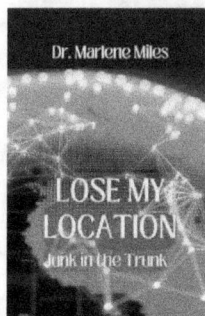

Man Safari, *The*

Marriage Ed. Rules of Engagement & Marriage

Made Perfect in Love

Motherboard (The) - soul prosperity series

Plantation Souls

Power Money: Nine Times the Tithe

The Power of Wealth *(forthcoming)*

Rules of Engagement & Marriage

Seasons of Grief

Seasons of War

Soul Prosperity soul prosperity series 3

https://a.co/d/5p8YvCN

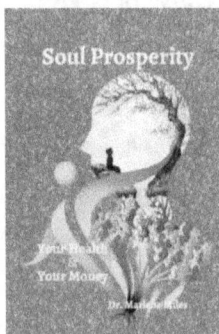

Souls Captivity soul prosperity series 2

The Spirit of Poverty

This Is NOT That: How to Keep Demons from Coming At You

Throne of Grace: Courtroom Prayer

Time Is of the Essence

Too Many Wives: *Why You Have Lady Problems*

Tormenting Spirits
https://a.co/d/dAogEJf

Triangular Power *(series)*

> Powers Above
>
> SUNBLOCK
>
> Do Not Swear by the Moon
>
> STARSTRUCK

Upgrade: How to Get Out of Survival Mode

Toxic Souls (Book 2 of series)

Legacy (Book 3 of series)

Warfare Prayer Against Beauty Curses
Warfare Prayer Against Poverty

When the Devourer is Rebuked

The Wilderness Romance *(series)*

- *The Social Wilderness*
- *The Sexual Wilderness*
- *The Spiritual Wilderness*

Credits:

Pastor Dr. Anthony O. Akerele, Mountain of Fire Virginia, *The Tree and Your Battles,* https://www.youtube.com/watch?v=sN2-NfpjfYY

Some prayer points adapted from **Prayer Rain** by Dr. Daniel Olukoya

Minister Joshua Orekhie

https://www.youtube.com/watch?v=i3z6_EyCIgs